BOOKS BY ERIC PANKEY

THE LATE ROMANCES   1997
APOCRYPHA   1991
HEARTWOOD   1988
FOR THE NEW YEAR   1984

The Late Romances

The Late Romances

POEMS BY

ERIC PANKEY

NEW YORK

ALFRED A KNOPF

1999

THIS IS A BORZOI BOOK
PUBLISHED BY ALFRED A. KNOPF, INC.

Copyright © 1997 by Eric Pankey

All rights reserved under International and Pan-American Copyright Conventions. Published in the United States by Alfred A. Knopf, Inc., New York, and simultaneously in Canada by Random House of Canada Limited, Toronto. Distributed by Random House, Inc., New York.

http://www.randomhouse.com/

The author gratefully acknowledges the editors of the following publications where these poems, many in earlier versions, first appeared:

The Agni Review: "Sworn Deposition"
The Bellingham Review: "Details"
Colorado Review: "Tulip"
Controlled Burn: "Borgo Antico," "For Now"
Delmar: "Fire," "In Heaven," "Prospero Returned From Exile"
Denver Quarterly: "To Christ our Lord"
DoubleTake: "A Feast in Jerusalem"
Gettysburg Review: "Study"
Grand Street: "The Pear as One Example"
Image: "The Crow's Complaint," "The Kingdom Likened to a Field of Weeds"
The Iowa Review: "Beyond Alchemy," "Savant of Birdcalls"
Kenyon Review: "Don Giovanni in Hell"
Lilt: "Interlude," "August Fugue"
Manoa: "Nostalgia"
The New England Review: "The Augury of Prospero," "The Dotage of Prospero," "Prospero Stays Home from Church"
New Letters: "Confession on the Island," "The Phrase of Thine Actions"
The New Yorker: "In Arcadia"
The Paris Review: "A Basket of Apricots"
Phoebe: "Homage"
Poetry: "Bric-a-brac," "June Vagaries," "The Grave of a Woman"
Quarry West: "At the Wapsipinicon River"
Seneca Review: "Two-Part Invention"
Sewanee Theological Review: "Detail from 'The Lamentation over the Dead Christ'," "Prayer," "Two Asides Beneath the New Moon"
The Southern Review: "After a Quarrel in Fiesole," "The Pilgrimage of my Father's Ghost," "Santo Spirito"
Sou'wester: "Testament"
TriQuarterly: "Melancholia"

Library of Congress Cataloging-in-Publication Data
Pankey, Eric.
    The late romances : poems / by Eric Pankey.
      p.   cm.
    ISBN 0-679-76605-7
    I. Title.
PS3566.A575L38   1997
811'.54—dc20   96-36676
                                                                     CIP

Manufactured in the United States of America
Published February 16, 1997
First Paperback Edition Published January 31, 1999

for Jennifer and Clare

Contents

Confession on the Island — 3

ONE

The Pear as One Example — 7
August Fugue — 8
Two Asides Beneath the New Moon — 9
In Heaven — 10
Tulip — 12
Don Giovanni in Hell — 13
Interlude — 19
June Vagaries — 20
The Pilgrimage of my Father's Ghost — 21
The Phrase of Thine Actions — 22
Details — 23
At the Wapsipinicon River — 24
To Christ our Lord — 25
Bric-a-brac — 26
The Kingdom Likened to a Field of Weeds — 27
Detail from "The Lamentation over the Dead Christ" — 28
The Grave of a Woman — 29
Study — 30
Fire — 31
Borgo Antico — 32
A Feast in Jerusalem — 33
Homage — 34
Prayer — 35
Beyond Alchemy — 36

Contents

TWO

Commedia	41
Santo Spirito	43
Two-Part Invention	44
Lines in Memory of my Father: Ponte Santa Trinità	45
Manifest Destiny	48
World Enough	49
The Crow's Complaint	50
Savant of Birdcalls	51
A Basket of Apricots	52
After a Quarrel in Fiesole	54
In Arcadia	55
Testament	56
Essays on a Lemon	57
Melancholia	58
Approaching Accademia: A Nocturne	59
Prospero Returned from Exile	60
Quartet	61
Prospero Stays Home from Church	63
For Now	64
Prospero Takes his Morning Coffee with the Conspirators	65
Sworn Deposition	66
In Siena, Prospero Reconsiders the Marriage at Cana	68
Nostalgia	69
The Augury of Prospero	70
Field of Vision	71
The Dotage of Prospero	72
NOTES	75
ACKNOWLEDGMENTS	76

The Late Romances

Confession on the Island

Bound to them in their bondage to me,
I was a slave to those I enslaved.
I split the tree that hived the honey,

But the swarm would not bequeath a taste.
I tied a knot that could not be slipped,
But the weather wore the ropes to threads.

There is no escape, no need to sound
The alarm. The harm I did I meant,
Even when I said I meant no harm.

Romance conceals a dark tragedy
Played out long before the play begins.
What good's revenge? It's a blade ground

And ground until it is a foil,
The good metal robbed for the point.
Here on this strange island forgiveness

Reigns. Each crime buffered by drollery
Seems only the mischief of children.
I've lived out my life in Eden

Believing it to be the World,
Believing I could reclaim the lost,
All that was forfeited to greed.

Yes, with my death I will pay my debt.
Like you, Spirit, I am indentured.
I am blessed you took pity on me.

ONE

The Pear as One Example

Light, the common denominator,
Does not conceive, but cloaks and covers,

And by wrapping reveals: the pick
Chips a sliver of ice; the wheat,

Shadow-swept by a storm front, glows gold;
The pear curves the lines the blinds let through.

Asked to name it, who would not say *pear*?
The plump and dimpled base, the blunt stem's

Woody accent, the green that is green.
He closes his eyes, closes his hand

Around the pear and says: This is it.
This I would know without metaphor.

But his touch rubs up the pear's perfume:
A hint of honey and magnolia,

Grape and almond. None of it the pear
But the otherness that is the pear.

And then his mind wanders to Eros:
Is it the unknown made intimate,

Or the known masked by light's flimsy veil?
When he opens his eyes to see

If what he holds is what he has held,
He holds what anyone would call a pear.

August Fugue

Rain, the last rain of evening, falls,
Unframed by the dark. The sound
Of rain as it falls sounds to them as sleep

Sounds: undisturbed, a slow weight
That drives a pendulum, what they hear
As the constant, the not-listened-for:

The sound that is their sleep, the rain
That falls. Which is beyond them and which
Within? They live. They live in indifference

And around them the last rain of evening falls.
She stands in the dark framed by the door
And hears the rain, without measure,

Unbound and precise, and when she turns
He turns and they give in to sleep. The rain,
Steady, clean, incises its fine shape

Against the dark. No scrape, no scratch
Mars the fall, the single declarative
Of its hush. She turns. He turns.

The rain is the sound that is their sleep.

Two Asides Beneath the New Moon

HE:

Shadows fill the shallow basin of the bay.
The water, calm after the wind has fallen,
Does not reflect the sky. The moon, worn thin
Last night, is now the somber cast of the earth.
No dim edge of lurid light bleeds from the edge.
Still, I can sense the new moon as a mass:
A broached surface, eclipsed and grave,
A conclave of gathered shade. How should I speak?
I know my words, words meant to illuminate
Can only conceal and leave us both dismal.
An alignment of bodies offers no more
Than adumbration, a dark toward which she turns
Away to sleep. Better to say nothing at all,
To let the tide in its turning churn and churn.

SHE:

If he asks if I'm asleep, should I answer?
The wide window frames all that is other,
All that is exterior and beyond us.
Tonight the moon lurks—there but not there—
A force brute and conspicuously hidden,
Colder than the depths out in the offing.
Some nights, the moon looms low, larger than the earth,
And we are fettered to its battered carapace.
What was once obscured is made palpable
In a grainy light that falls as ash falls.
How close then distance seems. We are two bodies,
Each in its way given shape by the other,
Each bound by the forces that hold us apart.
Good night, he'll say. Good night, I'll say. Good night.

In Heaven

If wind slashes through the honey locust,
A ragged bluster of blown rain and mist,

The limbs ride up and down in the squall.
They give in. Give in and do not resist.

If, on the windowsill, the redwing fritters
Away the storm with its cutthroat trill,

I listen, captive audience that I am,
Until it calms. The scald on its black wings—

A hot coal cut razor-thin and inlaid—
Seems an idol maker's fine tooling.

What good is an idol once its maker
Has shaped it? I have put my house in order

And can foresee the spare lines of its ruin:
An upright pillar, unpruned vines, violets

And poppies within the four right angles
Of this room. The roof beam like a shipwreck's mast

Still afloat beneath the overgrown grass.
Lightning bleaches the air. Still, the raw distance

Bleeds back as if it were nothing but shadow,
As if the *seen* were a flood that wells up

And over the split lip of a sinkhole,
Wells up from a deep sheath of perfect darkness.

In Heaven

And again the pattern completes itself—
The lightning's glare, the sudden dark, objects

Resettled and solid on the horizon—
Until I cannot discern invocation

From the certainty of perspective.
Who would have thought heaven a confinement,

An interior from which one looks always out,
A seraglio where velleity reigns,

Where one hears always the bride's offstage footsteps,
Her discreet approach? She never arrives.

Tulip

1.

Worthy Sovereign of Pandemonium,
Let the sultans fall and turbans unravel.
Let the parrot be your emissary.

2.

Yes, beauty soothes, but what one marries
Is its reprimand and its ruin: the house
Vacant, the dairy cows sold for slaughter.

3.

Poetry, however, is not a flower.
Who would speculate on a frill of words,
Offer as dowry the turn of a phrase?

4.

The cup, which once held tumult, holds
Nothing holy or worth a holy war.
Lord of Farce, make this tilled dirt your altar.

Don Giovanni in Hell

1. *To the Reader*

The owl and bell betray the hour.
This is my kingdom beyond boredom,
In which I am subject and object.

Desire requires a foretaste
Of loss. I require less and less.
Come, voyeur, be my guest. Rest assured

This is no apprenticeship in vice.
You see, there is no mastery, no
Perfection of corruption. Excess

Is excess. My own acquired taste.
Push your thumbs into the orange. Arrange
The bodies for ease of entry. Please

Yourself. Watch as the bruised flesh gives way.
Taste the salt as the slow writhing halts.
The perfume, the consuming sweetness

Never recedes. Like you I have needs,
But how to name them here where the same
Charred rose rises each day, how to act

Upon them? When the cobbles shift and sobs
From the catacombs enter your room,
Do you call that hell, my hypocrite?

Don Giovanni in Hell

    Be my guest among this ghostless mass.
    Here form blears and disowns its content.
    Repentance is all there is to repent.

    Pleasure? Pain? No. There is no measure.

    2. *The Body*

    The calipers pinch as they close on
    This slack form, this vehicle of lust,
    Still addled with use and so other.

    What did I expect, my God, from you?
    The resurrection of the body?
    The adagio of nostalgia?

    The wax, an oily ichor, spills down
    The candle's length. I cannot not
    Touch my finger to the hot liquid

    And when it cools, I peel it away.
    If only flesh were so easily
    Disposed of. But I am bound to it

    Like a worn horse to a whippletree.
    Who will untie the leather harness?
    Who will pull the pin from the clevis

    And let me drag my burden away?

Don Giovanni in Hell

3. *Ode on a Beet*

It is no heart but may as well be:
A loamy sweetness and brilliant mess
Bouyant on the dark mass of its own

Element. From here the purplish
Greens grow unseen, grow bitterer
In the hot air of the days above,

The heat of days that I once ruled.
Boiled, then quartered upon my plate,
It corroborates how my palate,

Now scalded, concedes to the subtle.
O for a valentine of cherry.
For the sticky ripe and stony pit.

But for one of little appetite
This pauper's diet is all that's needed,
A bloody show to sate the gut and heart.

4. *The Nostalgia of Don Giovanni*

Lord, I miss the gamut of birdsong.
The dismal haze that mackled the dawn.
The dissembling and the impasse.

The curtsy. The penitent kiss.
I miss the child's tears. The lifted veil.
The bluish gold that veins fine marble.

I miss the refrain of refusals.
The firm *no*. The elaborate stalls.
The raised blush at the mention of sin.

Don Giovanni in Hell

    I miss the face of each who gave in.
    The bleached bodice in place but unstrung.
    The host like a coin upon my tongue.

    The *noli me tangere*, the *why?*
    I have not forgotten each white lie.
    The moan of pleasure. The muttered *amen*.

    I was a ghost made flesh in women.

    5. *Ode to a Zucchini*

O uncouth squash, what is one to do?
One can pick at dusk and find at dawn
A clutch of needless fruit hard on the lawn.

Such blunt lengths without delicacy.
Abundance when one has grown weary
Of the crop. What the gardeners say

Is true: there's no giving it away.
The zucchini is one of God's two
Practical jokes. You know the other:

Between my legs, my prodigal brother.

Don Giovanni in Hell

6. *The Proverbs of Don Giovanni*

Don't squander the kindling on green wood.
A fool mistakes the heart for the choke.
A touch is worth a well-rhymed ballad.

For the crab every way is sideways.
For the one flattered nothing is false.
Even a devil can sing the old hymns.

Abstinence has no true opposite.
A pillager needs no accountant.
Lust is a wasp's nest burned as a torch.

Each garden hosts a hooded serpent.
Patience is dross; stealth a vein of gold.
How many stings is the honey worth?

7. *Elegy for Leporello*

Better a winding sheet and stone vault
Than a ditch and shovel's worth of lime.
Or to be taken whole as I was,

Rudely and without ceremony,
My mortal body dragged through the long
Shrill aria of everafter,

Where harmony dissolves to plainsong,
And plainsong to a metallic drone
Like the blue-throated hummingbird's whir

And furious standstill. Sleep now
My beloved accomplice, my shill.
The charnel house is your galleon.

Don Giovanni in Hell

    May forgiveness crown your pretty head.
    I would kiss your mouth, my lost double,
    If that would revive or redeem you.

    (To what good did my kiss ever come?)
    We lived as if we had shared a womb.
    Breech and premature, I blocked the way

    And thus I was plucked and you followed
    Through the open wound (*wide was the wound*).
    Lost is the comfort of that live crib.

    We were like the thieves who died with Christ,
    Like two brothers in a parable:
    Actors, allegorical figures,

    Leporello, but standing for what?

    8. *In Whose Image*

    Mine is a treasure of little use:
    A spilled universe of mustard seeds,
    The tedium of anything goes.

    There is time to be censured and rent,
    Time for rust to reave the relics,
    Time to envy God each he will take

    As his bride, each he must then ravish.
    I did what I could to mimic him,
    The God of my own exegesis,

    The God in whose image I am made.
    For all his loving, he is a brute.
    Grace, like a scythe, cuts what it cradles.

Interlude

Beneath the violet embellishment of trellised wisteria,
Day ends with the flash of a startled cardinal.
Isn't the world known by its conclusions? I ask you;

But you, standing in an alcove of late shade,
A figure incandescent, bright as the rosemary,
Will not break from the shadow and answer.

June Vagaries

Now the mourning dove vows a doubtful vow
And the redwing's rickrack of warning drags

Like a saw through the haze. The mockingbird's
Palaver—one part penny whistle,

One part warbler—idles in fits and starts.
The air is half fog, half honeysuckle,

And cold. What is ours and what is lent?
A wasp, all gold and lacquer, skims the glass.

A wasp lost in its thrum, bobs and glances,
Inflects its one sentence as a question.

The Pilgrimage of my Father's Ghost

Halfway home, he comes to the field's edge:
Deadfall, goldenrod, a moulder of uncut hay,
A rose-thicket hedgerow skirting the verge,

And beyond it, a decline into a ditch
That part of the year fills as a creek,
The water slow, moving beneath a smirched

Surface of algae and islands of leaf rot,
And the rest of the year, this: a dry furrow,
A nest of roots beneath the shale outcrop,

The cutbank steep where the curve sharpens.
The crab apple on the other side shimmers
As frost catches dawn and the day opens.

Bent, buckled, a snarl of dead and green wood,
The tree, he knows, is the tree he planted
And left to the will of suckers and bindweed.

What he has forgotten is the way over,
And as he struggles through the tangled thorns,
The sun, still cold, consumes him like a fever.

The Phrase of Thine Actions

What I know of the sacred is a gloss,
Words that will not translate into flesh.
The bread he broke is not his broken body,
But is a vernacular and homely trope.
A story retold is not the story told,
Yet his is the story I tell myself
No amount of retelling resolves.
I expected the audacity of bliss,
But was given the figures of sacrament,
The heavy curtain of allegories,
Words and acts that articulate his absence.
It is late summer, just before the harvest.
The gate— a trellis really for vines— is closed.
The way through covered with a floury dust.
What is dust that he would think to reshape it?

Details

As the fog lifts
The once-obscured is revealed as this—

The marsh island's ragged knoll,
The sandy spit of wild peas,

The crows perched in a dead oak.
Even from this distance, I see

Seed crowns, still wet, flare
As wind shuffles the grasses

And light strikes their yellowed lace,
Strikes and hammers the raw umber

To a frayed, overworked gold leaf
That tears and will not adhere

When the wind again shuffles the grasses.
The cold day, die cast

From fog's unsubstantial alloy,
Is tempered before my eyes.

The tipped strata of sky, treeline,
And black of oak is interrupted

By the level and plumb of roofs
And downspouts. The rows of windows,

Blank at this hour, hold what dark
The fog harbored. The seen-world,

Unreflected in that glass, for this instant,
Is this. Is this, this, this, and this.

At the Wapsipinicon River

(DAWN)

Through the gauze curtain of rain
That sweeps and dissolves into ground fog,
The plunge of a kingfisher flashes:

Taut, sheer, quick as a hammer falls,
Or a blade cuts and slips unseen
Into the parted. The bird is there

And isn't, caught in its instant,
Piece and afterpiece, flung like a flail,
A shade aswarm with gold flinders

That tears at the gray fringe,
That is and was and will be.

To Christ our Lord

A fire unhooks the snag
Of brambles. The seed crowns crack.
The rye grass, white traceries,
Shines and then crumbles to ash.
Only you would find comfort
In the habit of a vine,
In the smoke's bitter odor.
Soon a killing frost will check
The sap and the cricket cease
Its long deliberation.
The moon, a scrim of errors,
Will turn its back once again.
But you will not look away.
You love all things equally
And that is your flaw. Tell me,
What is love compared to shame?

Bric-a-brac

Say that sin is a seed that mildewed
Or scorched still germinates and prospers.
Or say that the end is prepared for.
The overture worked its sly magic.
When a phrase is next heard, we know it
And are pleased as it turns, when it turns,
Slow and brooding. We begin here: Here
Amid the bric-a-brac. Here inside
Amid order and fidelity.
The Day of Judgment is a day
Nonetheless, filled with laundry, errands.
The story, the story goes, starts
In innocence. It is morning.
There's no path hacked yet through the thicket.

The Kingdom Likened to a Field of Weeds

The green is not wheat, but mustard
That once sown flourishes to seed.
Wherever it falls, it takes hold.

The field, an indelible smear
Of darnel, thistle, and burdock,
Stinks of rank fullness and welter.

A swarm hovers like the wet smoke
Of an effigy set afire
And dragged across the brambled field.

Within its chirm and drone, crows turn.
The axle of the sun is locked.
No shade falls on the kingdom of weeds.

Detail from "The Lamentation over the Dead Christ"

The final gift that each affords
Is grief— requisite, not kindred—
A dismal freight as dense as gold.

As a body borne to its tomb
Is carried, so too they lift up
Their pain and leave it here with him.

It weighs upon him like a cloth
Infused in oils and spices,
A rancid balm bitter with ruth.

But she holds him as in her womb.
Now dread, not wonder, tinctures awe.
Once. Once she was alive with him.

The Grave of a Woman

All the flesh left is a patch of leather
Where the skull hollows. Each vertebra,
Like an ancient fish with open mouth
And ragged fin, holds its place in line.
The pelvis could be a worn mortar
And the scattered finger bones, gimcrack.
Do all who lie down expect to wake?

Consider the remains of this woman,
Buried in the gesture of sleep—
Her knees drawn up, one hand as a pillow.
Long ago the worms abandoned this trough.
Behold the kingdom that comes,
The earth the meek shall inherit.

Study

The wind. All things touched by wind.

The laurel, the little lamps of the tulip tree.
The crow, the gleaming crow,
Withholds its one thorny note,

A note that can rip a seam
From the mildewed canvas of dusk.

In the margins there are angels:

Scumble and crosshatch,
A smudge where a wing lodges
Against an earthly body.

Each a hurried sketch,
There in the margins.

The wind. Windfall. All things touched.
The wind preening the ragged cedar.
The wind mustering dust and debris.

The eye of an angel
Like the eye of a hawk when the hood is lifted.

Fire

Fire gnaws the green stems,
Inspires the backwash
Of smoke. It is the grind
And the stroke, the unchecked
Mint gone wild and sour
As the cicada's saw.
Fire resides in the straw,
In the milky candor
Of a woman's frescoed flesh.
Fire's a cathedral
In which the rosebud
Tips its miter. A snake's path
Winds through the colonnade.
A fast fuse. A loose thread.
But the needle is blunt
And cannot pierce the cloth.
Always in the story
Their father leads them deep
Into a wood. He leaves.
They mistake confection
For paradise. Father,
They call. Father. Father.
The chimney vents an ash
That tars the straight birches.
The wind is crazed with sparks.
Give us your word, Father,
Your blessed assurance.
Look. Look into the blaze:
How clean and white the glow.

Borgo Antico

Nothing is mercurial above the mid-day shadows
Or sallow. Noon's indigenous, heat-quickened clarity

Suffuses the ochre plaster, the aquamarine apse
Of sky, the green and cream-colored hills skirting the city.

What we reap is never the soul's true resurrected form,
But this bare kernel, this whole life kept whole within a husk.

We live in the body because it is flesh and is passing.
We live in the body because it is what we have to give.

A Feast in Jerusalem

Once as clear as ivory,
Blue like milk to the depths,
This face among the twelve,

A face like the others'
But now oxidized black,
A shade among the guests,

Seems the face of the one
Who betrays and fulfills,
Whose burden is the blame.

Unstable, the pigment,
Burned to its opposite,
Marks this one haloed head

As the guilty party,
Although all lean away
In disbelief and guilt.

Given the evidence,
We cannot help but judge,
Although the Judge sits there

And does not look to them
Or the one we accuse,
But into our eyes.

Homage

1.

O my God, looming and rough-hewn,
Forge me with rage. If this is the purge
Ferret out and scald the cold grub
Burrowed in at my heart. Let havoc
Consume its nest and larder.
Let your gold cauter stanch the wound.

2.

Fall inviolate sledge, and be known.
Blast away the sawdust and matchwood,
The ash-fall and rusted filings.
Let me be your wedge, let that edge
Gleam from use, burnished as it divides
The flawed from this hammerdressed world.

Prayer

Each day, adorned and in shambles, is your offering:
The shoreline's curved blade, worn and sharpened by the
   wave's rasp.

And inland, amid the hillside's olives and vineyards,
The fog's flesh ripped apart by wind, rendered and consumed.

And the iris. And the swarm and smoke that crowns the hive.
If only your heart were alive to the sweet center.

What do you love better: the ruin or its repair?
Desire's affliction or fire's harsh sacrament?

The stone walls of the orchard or the open gate out
Into this reliquary world? You will not answer,

You who see the cleft in all that is divisible.

Beyond Alchemy

1.

Always this half-light Old Ghost
As if a sheer curtain has blown down
Or a veneer of dust overlays the glass

One can still see and through to the other side
The hooded crow scavenges the hillside groves
Late heat shimmers off the roof tiles

If the rehearsed lines have been spoken
They cling like attar in the air
The spent iris dissolves and drips its ink

The sky tarnishes silver and olive
The silver of olive a silver
Like the thumb-smudge inside a mussel shell

Always this half-light to demarcate the rift
The precious the semi-precious the base
All beyond alchemy beyond change

Beyond Alchemy

   2.

Green on the ruddled roadside scree a lizard
Slips out of the recesses out and over
The tumbled grotto of debris out of sight

If the lesser kestrel passes like a shuttle
Between the umbrella pine and cypress
Between the stone barn and old city wall

Words will not unravel the fabric of its hunt
How does one distinguish between
A gift's burden and its intractable boon

Between fidelity and infidelity
Are words neither passage nor province
I will try Old Ghost try for once to stay quiet

To let the lost stay lost between static and rust
And not hoist the moon up not count on its dim
Chalk-drawn cast to reveal all you withhold

Beyond Alchemy

3.

Now half the fence is a screen of heart-shaped leaves
The vine finds another iron spear and coils
Should I take as sign or admonition

Its blind reaching out the way unchecked
It can take over an entire garden
Thrive and spoil as is the wont of things

The glut of silt and muck along the riverbank
Is a fester and ferment of mosquitoes
You Old Ghost you are the quiet one

And though you place a flock of starlings
In a tree at dusk a dark engine at work
Fueled by disquiet by agitation

You have not a single word to offer
Only your window overlooking is shuttered
How in a dumbshow does silence rebuke

TWO

Commedia

Besieged by nightfall, they fear
They have lost their direction.
The shapes night erases and conjures

Meld, at once foreign and familiar:
The upper rows of windows shuttered,
The facades blackened with soot and tar,

Ramshackle like a stone barn. Ask him,
He'll say they should turn around.
But she'll say, no, *that's* the way home,

(Where, of course, they left the map).
Twice already, they have passed
A pushcart rank with scraps of tripe.

They would settle for any landmark:
The Campanile's silhouette,
Ognissanti—Mannerist *and* Baroque—

Or, in the open shelter of a loggia,
Held up by Perseus as offering,
The lopped-off head of Medusa.

Stores they might have entered are grated.
Narrow streets narrow in the distance.
Somewhere beyond them, the tight, voluted

Whine of a vespa, headlight unlit,
Rattles through the city's high-walled maze.
The dark path it cuts snaps back shut.

Commedia

Annoyed, they do not snap or accuse,
But each wishes the other to be the one
At every corner who must choose

Right or left or straight ahead.
They walk a mile without talking.
All afternoon they had spent in bed

And then like children they had napped,
Only to wake at dusk and again
Make love. Both of them still hope

That this first day will be flawless.
So, utterly lost, they give up, give in,
And, to resolve the comedy, kiss.

Santo Spirito

Above the terra cotta roofs, swallows dart,
Stitching together the gathered dust of day.

At dawn, humidity hangs like a hive.
How surprised we are to find we live here,

Here within our bodies. The air, downswept,
Is fragrant: soot, sweat, spikes of lavender;

The unrestored light gold and aquamarine.
All is known and tenuous. Tenuous and known.

Bells. Then afterward, the quiet after bells.
Our bodies are not hidden, but revealed

Before the spirit of whom we are guests.
Revived, we hold each other and we rest.

Two-Part Invention

One should not love the grackle for its song,
Nor the pine for its flora. If one must,
The anvil may as well be an altar
And the loom, the scaffolding of heaven.
The invention of perfection was The Fall.
Still, one longs for discord and accords the flaw

Dominion over the whole. The rarest wool
Is not sheared, but gathered from thickets and thorns.
The fox is not cousin to the foxglove,
But the fox has its hole and the crow its nest.
The crow and the grackle wear the thunder's rags.
If God is a word, then words sally us forth.

Lines in Memory of My Father: Ponte Santa Trinità

Water tarnishes
Green and cinnabar
A slosh against gravel

A shrunken river
A narrow rift
A poor excuse

But reason enough
For the stone bridge
That holds me up

If I am to judge
Nothing before the time
Until the Lord comes

Who both will bring
To light the hidden things
Of darkness and will make

Manifest the counsels
Of the heart then
Let me wait here

As heartless as he accused
Crippled by stroke
One half of his body

Dragged the other half
Across the waiting room
Just to hold me

Lines in Memory of my Father: Ponte Santa Trinità

        His right hand lugged his left
        Up to my shoulder
        And he leaned against me

        The half-dead weight
        Of his embrace
        Causing me to step back

        And lean closer
        Stumble and buttress
        Through the awkward dance

        Both of us old
        Before our time
        And each blaming the other

        A poor excuse
        Is as good as you get
        He'd say and true

        Or not he said it
        The spirit here
        Is the river

        Moving and still
        Slow after weeks of heat
        Or at its will

        With flood it continues
        Half-way through his life
        He cried *my god*

        And fell with a thud
        To his bedroom floor
        I'll stay here on this bridge

Lines in Memory of my Father: Ponte Santa Trinità

In a city of churches
And let Jesus
Bent over his brood

Hang as unredeemed
As any man strapped
To a body in pain

I can live with it
My father said
Meaning he'd rather not

Manifest Destiny

Where his left hand fulcrums the shaft
And where at the tip his right hand
Levers the weight, the shovel's ash
Is worn to a sheen, rubbed silver
As he cleaves and lifts the sandy earth.
What bears no work is smudged by rust:
The abutment's curled-back metal,
The socket and its blunt rivets.
His hands, roughed and calloused, are not
As hard as the wood they wear down.
American that he is, he knows
All he touches is changed for good.

World Enough

Here the garlic is a lily
And the common pigeon a dove.

The bud of the peony—
Green, waxy, white in the seam crack—

Is world enough to behold,
Yet from that globe

Fullness swells, rose-like, tatter-edged.
What is faith but the restless hope

That the hidden will be opened?
A rake nudges ash to ember.

The blurred head of a woodpecker
Pinpoints the grub beneath the bark.

The scrabble of a pickax
Reveals rock beneath rock,

A hardness that will not be budged
By the tool brought to bear.

The Crow's Complaint

    Beneath the rain, the crow
Lifts from the flooded creek.
    A snake
        caught in its beak

    Squirms, uncoils, and throws
The bird off-balance. Then
    The wind
        changes and sends

    The bird swooping back low
Against the bank, headfirst
    And worse,
        the dropped snake, lost

    In the grass, finds a hole
To slither down. The crow
    Then crows
        the caw it knows.

    Loud above the snake's hole,
The bird spreads its wings, struts
    And lets
        no one forget

    Its loss. Bright as wet coal,
It parts its yellow beak
    And shrieks
        and shrieks and shrieks.

    The snake knows what it knows:
The hole's a perfect fit.
    It waits,
        uncharmed. Stays put.

Savant of Birdcalls

The blue herons' do-si-do,
The barn swallow's wheel, the hawk's

Fell swoop, the kingfisher's fall:
Who but me taught them to dance?

From my roost, I still dictate
The show of the peacock's fan—

A gaudy display unfurled
Infrequently with a squawk.

I taunt the owl with my hoot
And shake the crows from the trees.

I, the savant of birdcalls,
Out-mimic the mockingbird.

The cuckoo's wooden coo-coo,
The osprey's exhausted screech

And the cardinal's interval
Are, in my throat, native sound.

Call me duck, dodo, or dove,
Plagiarist or perjurer.

I don't, as the bobwhite does,
Question the truth of my name.

A Basket of Apricots

Flustered (words always made him flustered),
He thought of saying never mind, but instead
Changed the subject. She, the listener, listened

As he turned away from his confession.
She wondered why he should feel so ill at ease
Describing, now, a basket of apricots

That had been set down in the square of sunlight
Between them. How he went on: *blush, fragrant suede,*
Declivity, the hidden burled pit, . . .!

All of it seemed overwrought and wrong to her.
Angry, she thought him a fool. And he, too,
Grew angry and said, You never listen.

To what, she said, What are you saying to me?
By then she could not look at him. She watched
The smudges of gnats hover above the fruit.

Next, he might call the sunlight *gold lamé*.
Next—who knows what he might say next, and worse,
She thought, what he means? Then, when he mentioned

The sunlight, which she had to admit
Was lustrous and at this point a way to change
The subject, she laughed, willing to forgive.

But that laugh pricked him and he said, Never mind.
What he had first meant to say now seemed so clear
That he felt like blurting it out. There, he'd say.

A Basket of Apricots

But however he phrased it to himself,
Imagining her as the listener,
It seemed hardly worth saying. There? she'd say back,

As if to throw out the evidence he'd entered.
The gnats, bouyed on the too-sweet air, brought to mind
Lines from Shakespeare he thought to recite:

"Who can . . . / Cloy the hungry edge of appetite
By bare imagination of a feast?"
For both their sakes he thought the better of it.

And when she lifted her hand from her lap, he hoped
She would reach across the table to hold his hand.
But she slapped at the air and shooed away the gnats.

After a Quarrel in Fiesole

Kindled by the cicada's worn-down flint,
The heat lasts through to evening.

The pines gutter, then flare, the spindly pines
Through which the wind is pulled into thread.

If we can possess only what we will renounce,
Imagine all we will finally lose.

The straw is already gold and thrown down
On the rutted trail that tends to flood,

One of two trails back down to town,
One of two, but neither is easy.

In Arcadia

Half buried in scrub and red poppies
And half exhumed, the barren half-moon

Of the threshing floor, fissured and chipped,
Is bleached the white of lime, of the moon

Itself, full last night, instructed in light,
In chapters of light as wordless as

The owl's wing. Not yet noon, the sun hangs,
Worn and burnished from use, like a heart

Made of glare and ember. The mint spreads
Its mineral flame down the hillside.

Amid the green, the lizard's tongue flicks,
A *Y* of blood divining the air,

There and gone. There and gone. There.

Testament

How far and how keenly the causeway cuts,
Like a surveyor's string taut in moonlight,

Separating one body from its twin.
All traffic follows that thin line

Between one green expanse and another.
What can I offer you, love, but weather

And local flora as testimony?
And as an image of matrimony

This wide water divided: one but two?
The iris and beach pea bloom more red than blue,

But blue is the base— part sky, part ocean.
How tense the surface after the rain ends.

The moon, halfway through its phases, doubles
On water not calm, but untroubled.

Essays on a Lemon

1.

Violet shadow. A blur
That darkens where it touches
The curved outskirts of the real.

2.

Pine resin and basil. Thyme
And turned earth: no concoction
Counterfeits the prime of zest.

3.

From the lexicon of salt,
One word transfigures the sting,
The resonant hiss of the clear.

4.

What could mar the sun's surface?
Not bay, or the poppy seed's
Blue. O ripeness, O glare.

5.

The lemon reveals itself
Only in the rare dusk-light.
It reveals only itself.

Melancholia

Removed from its axle, the chipped grindstone,
A useless mass, leans against the wall.
Above, scales hang on a hook, balanced and empty.

Half the sand has slipped as time to the bottom.
The bell, unrung, will not be rung at the hour:
The plumb bob of its brass clapper unmoved,

The glinting lip unshimmered into music.
The moulding plane, handsaw, and scattered nails
Rest, idle, spoiled for want of occupation

At the brooding angel's feet. A mold of rust
Waits to pock the polished edges and points.
As if the practical text of her neglect,

The book, clasped shut on her lap, remains unread:
The pages never dog-eared, the spine unbroken.
If she could bring a single hope to light

And not cast it aside in the dull allure
Of twilight and moonlight that overshadows all,
If she could unfurl her wings and imagine flight,

And allow the thought of flight to rise up
Without the ballast of set squares and compasses,
Or the marble globe that has rolled onto the floor,

Then she might see that beyond the clutter and forms,
Beyond the unrendered distance into which she stares,
All one is ever given is *this* clutter, *these* forms,

That distance to arrange and in arranging change.

Approaching Accademia: A Nocturne

It gets dark while they talk.
The vaporetto, almost empty,
Crosses the water. Revs, then balks,

Bangs against the landing stage.
As a rope creaks taut, she stops
Midsentence: the smudged vestiges

Of balconies, alcoves, and arches
And the running lights, drawn like oxgall,
Marble on the canal's inverted *S*.

He sees for once what she sees,
And seeing it, as through her eyes,
Knows her heart, or so he believes.

The loose, unraveled braids of the wake
And opaque green of the flat surface
Are rubbed up argentine as dusk

Deepens the canal. Domes and spires,
A string of white party lights,
A bridge's underside, and belltowers

All blur on the water's reaches,
Unfurl and glissade from berth to berth,
As the slack rope unknots and releases.

Prospero Returned from Exile

He cursed the flinty soil and a fig tree grew.
He praised the magpie and suffered its harangue.
He hawked his scorious heart as scrap metal,

But no forge's blast could smelt a precious ounce.
How deep his books fell as ballast he could not say,
But little by little the silt has settled,

At last, the matter of his obsolete art.
So long to the cusp of the crab's claw.
So long to the fortified wall mottled with soot.

So long to the scarecrow strung on a gibbet.
So long to the spleenwort, to the jackdaw's withdrawal . . . .
His farewells stretched as long as his daughter's prayers,

In which each soul is given quarter and comfort,
As on a frescoed "Last Judgment" he half remembered:
What must have been Hell is in ruin, effaced,

Scraped over with gray plaster to keep the wall intact.
Paradise floats above the rough repair,
An island to which all are pulled safe ashore.

Quartet

All morning the song of a pulley's creak
The mortar's gravel scrape against the trowl

The blade's belltone tapping a brick into place
Snared in a fringe of leaf-shadow the sun

Bears down nonetheless against the green shutters
Closed at this hour when the racket ceases

Those who made this world are returning home
Far off someone whistles or a blackbird calls

*

The plaster facade tinctured with rust moulders
The clotheslines unburdened hang slack in the breeze

Like a gold filament a bit of chaff
Tossed on an updraft flickers on and off

Memory like mother-of-pearl births
And swallows all available light

Sometimes a touch sometimes total immersion
The cool of these sheets afternoons and nights

Quartet

        *

House martins bank over the water and swoop
A filigree of flight doubled in the depth

Loops that list on the surface and vanish
On this first day of a pilgrimage

How could one denounce the world's transcience
Light or *shadow* when neither is *presence*

Nor *absence* in this last remnant of evening
As martins retreat to nests beneath the bridge

        *

If the honey and wormwood tasted the same
Would he forget sweetness or bitterness first

One pink cloud like a hand-hewn slab of marble
Like the tipped lid of the Holy Sepulcher

In Duccio's "Three Marys at the Tomb"
Hangs unmoved above the angles of tiled roofs

Unmoved by the frail shoulder of the wind
Until he looks again and finds it gone

Prospero Stays Home from Church

What if he called a thousand miles *arrival*
And let an egret rip out the fog's hem?

What if he started over again, one stitch at a time?
The dawn, gray as a whetstone, is cold.

A mud dauber worries over its grotto
Anchored in the slate eaves. All work is patchwork.

The wine left open on the table has turned.
Out of muck, haze, and low tide mire,

A demiurge might muster the wherewithal
To shape a world. Maybe he'd need some straw.

Maybe an anvil. Spit and dust to make a slip.
An old Sabbath breaker, he'd never rest

Until he fashioned from his disregard
Both the keen edge of a pruning hook

And something duller, like a human heart.
Until he conceived from his furrowed brow

Bach, and therefore *The Art of the Fugue*.

For Now

For now, he prefers *adagio* to *presto*.
The blue, resinous perfume of rosemary
To the magnolia's velvet buds.

Someday he will learn to abandon
The unsubtle harmonies
But for now his hands reach for the chords
He learned to hear long ago as music:
His right igniting the single torch flare
In the sky of a chiaroscuro nocturne,
His left raising Christ above the toppled guards,
Who sleep through heat lightning's rumble and static.

For now, content with the present tense,
Swept clean of what-might-have-been—
Rumors and misplaced documents—
He can almost swallow the grit of a cry
Balanced like a pearl on his tongue.

Prospero Takes his Morning Coffee with the Conspirators

This morning a trail of spots mars the sun
Like gall on the surface of molten glass.
He closes his eyes to read the after-image:

A luminous archipelago,
An exposed refuge on a storm-stirred sea.
With his eyes still closed that image fades,

And its blankness shimmers to a silver
As bright as a telescope's speculum.
On it he sees the palms' fan traceries,

The shore's ambit skirted with sargassum,
Nets hung up to dry, and a cave's opening.
His friends assure him there was never a skiff

On which he was cut adrift. No conspiracy.
We are the ones, in fact, who rescued you.
All you have ever conjured is this story.

When Prospero starts in on his story,
As he does each morning over coffee
In the stark glare of the piazza,

They notice for the first time his eyes are closed.
They speculate at what wonders he must see.
(Half of magic, he's learned, is distraction.)

Entranced by the tale's lulls and intricacies,
They sit and listen. The coffee grows cold.
They open their own eyes. Find the old man gone.

Find themselves lost, wrecked on his words.

Sworn Deposition

What he remembers holds like a slipknot,
So that whether the tide nudged in or out,

Or if black mud marbled the sand, or rain,
A downpour, lugged its weight through the pines,

Does not matter: each moment caught or released,
Each moment overlaid by the next, embossed,

Watermarked, is never whole but detail:
Happenstance, not incarnation; rubble,

Not ransom. No, he cannot distinguish
Truth from half-truth, the peck of a goodnight kiss

From seduction, the well-made original
From the restoration's flaws. He recalls

Halfway through his testimony the logic
By which he had hoped to proceed. A wreck

Is what he has made of this and will of that.
Loving the flesh but forgetting the pit,

He sinks his teeth in. If he could play the Fool
With overripe buffoonery and skill,

Remember to say what both conceals and cuts,
Advises and mocks, with love and bitter wit,

And not always reply in this taut tenor,
A player who is always an amateur,

Sworn Deposition

His love of the act might increase more than love.
But he is under oath and must behave.

What he has forgotten he has forgotten.
The lees stirred up settle back to the bottom:

Dregs on dregs, varve on varve, the sediment
Becoming, over time, a firmament

On which the life he lives is enacted.
Read back his answer, he cannot retract it.

In Siena, Prospero Reconsiders the Marriage at Cana

All sleight-of-hand trails the dross and clutter
Of the unseen, clumsily like an anchor,
Barely concealing its means as it deceives.

What else can be made of signs and wonders
But close readings and a display of awe?
What is left when the waited-upon is fulfilled?

After the standoff Jesus conjures a trick.
Should such an act be enacted knowing
The *next* and the *next* will be demanded?

Of course, he one-ups himself, causes a fuss,
And the story plunges headlong to finale.
And then encore. Above, in the Sienese heat,

A pair of ravens patrol the parapet.
Washed linens flap on the clothesline.
A shadow bisects the curved blade of the Campo.

As if in confirmation of a miracle,
The twisted olive bears the wind's history,
A gnarl that hinders the brisk disorder,

Renders it as the unmoved here and now.
Skittish pigeons clatter up in the air.
Into shadow. Out of shadow. And then back down.

And no one, not even God, lifted a finger.

Nostalgia

Afterward, it was hard to sleep at night
With only the hiss of the possum
And the mole's dull progress to fill the stillness.

The owl's talons closed too quietly on the vole.
After rain, wind brought down the rain in the trees,
But neither a storm nor the *drip, drip* repaired

The material of experience,
The unmendable rent of what is withheld.
What is the Word that it remains silent

Here in the impasse after creation,
Where he wakes, startled by a voice, and awake
Finds his own mouth formed around an unsayable word?

The Augury of Prospero

In the split-open breast of the lamb,
He fails to read the deity's will.
With his stick, he pokes at the carcass.

He nudges the wreckage of ribcage
Aside as if the Truth were concealed
In the sealed-off chambers of the heart,

In the intricacies of marrow
Or the maze and switchbacks of the bowels.
He sees what he always sees: the past,

The unattended moments festered,
Bloated with all that was left unsaid,
Images haunting abstract spaces.

He stares at the cracked shoulder socket
And parses out its function and flaw.
By the time he glosses each sinew,

He has butchered the sacrificed beast
And makes a feast of his misreading.

Field of Vision

Overwhelmed by rain, by that cross-grain of cold,
The flooded salt marsh is a raw verdant slash,
A surface turbulent, shuddered by each gust.

Whether the downpour quickens, or wind slackens,
The window's *retablo* reflects and distorts
This vessel of shadows, this featureless face

That hovers among what is cast and imposed
Upon the storm-swamped depth of the dark window:
A self-portrait through which he must look to see.

The Dotage of Prospero

Untouched by his craft or alchemy,
The twin snakes coupling in the vineyard
Rub up a music the wind sluices away.
In the dusk heat, he drags out a folding chair
And surveys the garden he has reclaimed.
A porcupine digs in the iris bed,
Wedges in, shoulder-deep, head hidden.
Bored by a whole day of letting things be,
The old man, slumped in his chair, kicks at gravel.
The porcupine flares its quills, all threat,
And scuttles off into the undergrowth.
Exhausted from his triumph, the old man
Nods and dozes, dozes and nods.
Spirit, he mumbles from the strand of a dream
And though not invoked, a tawny owl
Falls from the umbrella pine's shadowed island,
Falls then lifts silently on the night's hot air.

NOTES

The following poems owe a debt to these sources: "Confession on the Island": Wallace Stevens, "Credences of Summer"; "In Heaven": *Habakkuk*, 2:18–20; "Tulip": Zbigniew Herbert, *Still Life with Bridle*; "Don Giovanni in Hell": Charles Baudelaire, "Au Lecteur," John Milton, *Paradise Lost*, Book VIII, Donald Justice, "Two Songs from *Don Juan in Hell*," Jack Gilbert, "Don Giovanni on His Way to Hell"; "Interlude": Eugenio Montale, "Sul Llobregat," Emily Dickinson, #501; "The Phrase of Thine Action": Cynthia Griffin Wolff, *Emily Dickinson*, John Donne, *Devotions*, XIX; "The Kingdom Likened to a Field of Weeds": John Dominic Crossan, *The Historical Jesus*; "Lines in Memory of My Father: Ponte Santa Trinità": *1 Corinthians* 4:3–5; "Melancholia": Raymond Klibansky, Erwin Panofsky, & Fritz Saxl, *Saturn and Melancholy*, Albrecht Dürer, "Melancolia I", Engraving, 1516; "Quartet": Eugenio Montale, "Lindau," Eugenio Montale, "Ossi di seppia"; "Nostalgia": George Santayana, *Interpretations of Poetry and Religion*.

The following poems are dedicated as follows: "Interlude" to Jan Weissmiller; "At the Wapsipinicon River" to Bob Crum and Marjorie Sandor; "Study" to Charles Wright; "Santo Spirito" to Jennifer Atkinson.

ACKNOWLEDGMENTS

Thanks to Jane and Robert Atkinson for the use of their house summer after summer in Old Saybrook, Connecticut, where most of these poems were begun. Thanks to Harry Ford for his support and encouragement. Sincere thanks to Jennifer Atkinson, Allison Funk, Jeff Hamilton, Steven Schreiner, and Jason Sommer, whose friendship, attention, patience, and good advice sustained me as these poems were being written.

A NOTE ABOUT THE AUTHOR

Eric Pankey was educated at the University of Missouri and the University of Iowa. His first book of poems, *For the New Year*, received the Academy of American Poets' Walt Whitman Award in 1984. His second book, *Heartwood*, was published in 1988 and his third, *Apocrypha*, in 1991. He has received grants from the Ingram Merrill Foundation and the National Endowment for the Arts. He lives in Fairfax, Virginia, where he teaches at George Mason University.

A NOTE ON THE TYPE

The text of this book is set in Waverley, introduced by the Intertype Corporation in 1941, and named for the hero of Sir Walter Scott's novel. In actuality it is very close to Walbaum, named for Justus Erich Walbaum, a type founder at Goslar and Weimar in the late eighteenth and early nineteenth century, whose type was introduced into England in the 1920's and made available worldwide by the Monotype Corporation. Aside from a certain heaviness of the Waverley (as opposed to the crisp lightness of Walbaum), there are very few details in which they differ.

COMPOSITION BY HERITAGE PRINTERS, INC.,
CHARLOTTE, NORTH CAROLINA

PRINTED AND BOUND BY QUEBECOR PRINTING
KINGSPORT, TENNESSEE

DESIGNED BY HARRY FORD